# Latitude 54

## The story of the Karran fleet
## of Castletown, Isle of Man

## Billy Stowell

*Billy Stowell.*

*Dedicated to my Mother,
Peggy.*

Published by
B. Stowell

with the assistance of
The Manx Heritage Foundation

Printed by
The Copy Shop
48 Bucks Road, Douglas

Painting of the Manx King
on the cover painted by
Mr John Halsall

Photographic images curtesy
of Rob & Peter Karran

ISBN No. 978-0-9567393-0-8

"Crossing the line (Equator)" with Neptune

# Preface

It is quite commonplace these days for a book to be introduced with the words 'based on a true story.' This book is not one of them. Instead, this is a collection of information which records one family's fleet of merchant ships that traded internationally from 1860 until 1913. The family were Manx[1] and their name was Karran.

The fleet's home island, the Isle of Man, boasts many interesting chapters in maritime history. The Vikings - attracted by the island's central position in the Irish Sea (from which they could launch attacks on other coastal areas) - settled throughout the island, introducing their pioneering nautical skills to the Manxman. Later, the island thrived on its hugely successful fishing industry, and hundreds of boats were built on the island. In 1830, the Isle of Man Steam Packet Company commenced business, providing an Irish Sea ferry service that still runs today.

One of the island's more famous residents – Sir William Hillary – was a resident of Douglas when he founded the Royal National Lifeboat Institution[2] in 1824.

It is also interesting to note that the oldest ship in the world that is still seaworthy, the barque, *Star of India*, is now a sailing museum based in San Diego, California, though she was originally built in 1863 at Ramsey, Isle of Man.

---

[1] Manx is both the nationality and language of the people of the Isle of Man, which is situated in the Irish Sea between England, Ireland, Scotland and Wales.
[2] For the first 30 years, the RNLI was called the National Institution for the Preservation of Life from Shipwreck.

Although a lot of information has been recorded concerning the island's maritime past, sadly only a comparatively small amount of material regarding the history of the Karran fleet has been recorded, though invaluable documentation has been preserved in the memoirs of both Tom Karran and his sister, Tessa (both of whom were children of Captain George Karran, who played an integral part in the history of the fleet), and in the writings of individual historians.

I have taken the opportunity to study original texts, searched nautical publications, and talked to some of the quayside characters of Castletown (the fleet's port of registration) to discover snippets of information that have been passed down through the generations, in order to glean as much knowledge that I could about the Karran fleet. This book, however, has never been intended to be regarded as the definitive compilation of data regarding this subject.

I have also had the good fortune to meet two of the Karran family's current generation, Peter and Rob.

As time went on, I started to feel as if I knew the people involved so long ago in this fleet's adventures, and now I hope the reader can enjoy the same experience.

*Billy Stowell*

Sailors Aloft

# Nautical Terminology

For the benefit of the reader not familiar with the terminology used in this book to describe the various sail rigs and nautical terms, a basic explanation is provided here:

- **'Fore and aft'** refers to any objects aboard (e.g. sails etc) that are rigged or fitted to masts in line lengthways to the ship.

- A **'fore and aft schooner'** is a vessel rigged fore and aft.

- A **'brig'** has two masts (square rigged – i.e. sails that are set at right angles to the ship), but the mainsail on the after mast is fore and aft.

- A **'topsail schooner'** is schooner rigged, but has one square rigged sail on the higher part of its foremast.

- A **'barque'** has three or four masts square rigged, except the sails on the after mast are fore and aft.

- A sailing **'ship'** is a vessel with three or four masts, square rigged on all.

- The **'beam'** measurement of a vessel is the width of the ship.

- The **'draught'** of a vessel is its depth below the waterline.

- **'Freeboard'** is the distance from a ship's waterline to the main or upper deck.

- **'Gross tonnage'** is a measure of the internal capacity of a vessel. It is calculated by dividing the total internal volume in cubic feet by 100.

- **'Net tonnage'** is the vessel's gross tonnage minus any crew spaces, anchor cable lockers, engine rooms etc. Thus it is the space available for cargo or passengers.

- **'Longitude'** is a measure of how far east or west a point on the globe lies counting from 0° to 180° East or West. The Prime Meridian (0°) is a line running from Pole to Pole through Greenwich near London, England. Degrees are subdivided into Minutes and Seconds.

- **'Latitude'** is a measure of how far one is north or south of the Equator. The Equator is Latitude 0° and the North Pole is at 90° North. The further south one goes, the higher the latitude number until one reaches 90° S at the South Pole.

Livestock

Reeling in the Logline

Streaming the Logline
To Calculate the ship's speed,
one end of the Logline would
be thrown overboard.
As the ship moved forward knots in the line would be
counted as they passed over the ship's rail.
Notice the glass sand timer that was used to calculate
the ship's speed in 'Knots'

Capt. Robert Karran     Capt. Tom Karran     Capt. George Karran

Tilly Karran

Karren Line Captain's Badge

Family sketch of Tess Karran
Date estimated 1895

# A Birth at Sea

In March 1891, a sailing ship, the *Manx King*, was on passage from the Atlantic towards the Pacific, bound for San Francisco. As it would be another twenty-three years before the Panama Canal would open for commercial shipping, the notoriously dangerous sea route around the tip of South America still had to be negotiated by the hardy crew of the *Manx King*.

Bad visibility and, consequently, the absence of celestial navigational fixes resulted in the *Manx King* being further south than she should have been. The vessel was in danger of hitting ice when, providentially, a brief window of improved visibility allowed Captain Karran to observe the sun, enabling him to obtain a sextant reading that revealed their latitude: below sixty degrees South. With renewed confidence he steered further northwest.

It was not unheard of in those days, especially on family-owned ships, for the ship's master to be accompanied by his wife and children. Captain George Karran was no exception. Tilly[3], his wife, and their two year old son, Tom[4], were aboard for the voyage. On 24th March, 1891, they had reached 54°12'16" South, 73°35'14" West. It was here that Tilly gave birth to their second child, a baby girl who they named Tessa[5].

Ten days later, still in rough conditions and trying to get further west to alter onto a more northerly course, the ship experienced hurricane force winds and all but capsized. As sailors would say, she was 'on her beam ends.' The cabins were awash with seawater that had poured in through the deck skylights, and the water was rising at a rapid and frightening pace. It is a credit to the skill of the Manx sailors aboard, and the craftsmanship of the Stockton builders (who built the ship), that *Manx King* was righted and survived the storm to enter the Pacific Ocean. The ship called at Valparaiso, Chile, and from there sailed onwards to San Francisco, where little Tessa was christened. Her middle name 'Aloha' was in honour of King Bowler of Hawaii, a friend of the Captain and his wife. Captain Karran would have noticed the coincidence of the latitude of his daughter's birthplace, 54° 12' South, as Latitude 54° 12' North passes through the Isle of Man, an island in the centre of the Irish Sea, and the homeland of the Karran family.

We will return to the *Manx King* and her crew later in this book, but for now we must go further back in time - 31 years - to the birth of the Karran fleet.

[3] Matilda May Wolfe Clarke Karran
[4] Thomas William Karran
[5] Theresa Aloha Karran

# ENIGMA

*Built 1845    Wrecked 1922*
*Length 76 Feet    Beam 19 Feet*
*84 Ton*

In 1845 the brig, *Enigma*, was launched on the Hooghli River, Calcutta, India. She is recorded to have been built of 'the stoutest timber procurable.' Her strakes (planking) were teak, and her rib-frames were of a hard Indian wood, copper fastened and built for speed. The vessel's figurehead was a bird with fish scales, indeed an enigma.

The *Enigma* was an opium runner, though it has also been recorded that she was a 'slaver' and most likely carrying slaves in the Indian Ocean.[6] She was heavily armed with sixteen guns, seven each side, and two long swivel 'stern chasers' housed aft. A heavily armed crew were always aboard. It could be said that she was little better than a pirate vessel. Indeed, it is odd today to think that most Europeans of that time would have regarded the shameful slave and opium trades as respectable.

India had been colonised since the eighteenth century and quickly became the centre of Britain's impressive trade network. For centuries India had been a producer of opium, and this narcotic became one of her main exports as, during its Imperial rule, Britain forced China to allow India to have a monopoly on the opium trade. But as with most drug related affairs, events soon took a darker turn. Despite China's prohibition laws, the British were soon employing Chinese opium dealers to encourage Chinese officials to use the drug, in the hope of widespread addiction. By the mid 1830s, about one percent of the Chinese population were addicted to opium and its derivatives, though in the coastal areas where smuggling occurred the number of people addicted to the same drug was estimated to be as high as ninety percent. By 1836, opium shipped from India to China was feeding the habit of twelve million addicts. The Indian Government prospered.

An attempt by the Chinese government to stop the flood of opium into its country led to a series of conflicts between Britain and China which became known as the *Opium Wars*. China was defeated in these wars and, subsequently, Britain forced the Chinese Government to sign the *Treaty of Nanking*, which established the 'treaty ports' that would control the drugs being imported into China (though it took officials until 1860 before the compromise was fully established).

It is not on record whether the *Enigma* operated on this opium trade under licence, or carried on in the traditional way of smuggling, but the latter cannot be ruled out.

In 1860, when *Enigma* was fifteen years old, she voyaged to London carrying a shipment of general cargo. From there, on passage to Glasgow, she encountered a storm in the Irish Sea and took shelter in

---

[6] Source: Pacific Steam & Navigation Company's publication Sea Breezes, Volume 13, 1929

the thriving fishing port of Peel[7] on the Isle of Man. Here she was immediately seized by the Coroner[8] for unpaid debts and put up for sale by public auction.

A Manxman, John Karran, father of Captain George Karran, became the *Enigma's* new owner and, with this purchase, founded the Karran fleet. His son, Tom, took command of the vessel, mostly on Baltic or Spanish cargoes. The vessel was eventually sold to Mr Joseph Qualtrough, a shipbuilder of Castletown, Isle of Man.

By 1877, *Enigma* was owned by J. Watterson of Port St Mary, Isle of Man. On passage from Glasgow to Dun Laoghaire in Ireland with a load of coal, the tide stranded her on the east side of Holy Island, Lamlash Bay, in the Clyde Estuary. It was reported that she was feared to be a total loss[9], though Captain Corkill and his three crew evidently succeeded in refloating her, because she went on working for a further forty-five years after this brush with disaster.

Coal taken from Whitehaven or Glasgow to Irish and Manx ports appears to have been the *Enigma's* main trade, although many other cargoes - such as salt, gravel, grain etc - were shipped on Irish Sea routes.

In 1913, *Enigma* changed hands to owners on the Solway Firth, first at Dalbeattie and later at Whitehaven. During one of her changes of ownership, she was altered from brig rig to schooner rig.

On 5th December 1922, she was carrying a load of coal from Whitehaven to Garlieston, on the north side of the Solway, when, three miles SSW of the Isle of Heston, she was lost with all hands[10]. Skipper Pearson and deck-hands Robert Marsden and James Quirk of Douglas, Isle of Man, were all recorded as lost. The *Enigma* was nearly eighty years old when she went down.

By 1870 the Karran family were purchasing other vessels of comparatively small tonnage. John Karran (who as stated earlier was the founder of the family fleet) had six sons, three of which - Thomas, Robert and George - had embarked on successful careers at sea, after learning basic navigation skills at a School of Navigation run by the one-armed Capt. Tom Watterson[11]. Another son, Edward, had qualified as a Master Mariner. Edward decided not to follow his brothers into careers at sea,

---

[7] To learn more about Peel, visit the House of Manannan and the Leece Museum (both in Peel), or view their websites on the internet.
[8] Under Manx law a coroner is an executive officer of the Manx High Court, similar to a sheriff or bailiff in England and Wales.
[9] Source: Shipping Intelligence LL no 19650, London, Wednesday April 18 {1877]. See also PP Abstracts Returns of Wrecks and Casualties on Coasts of the UK 1876-77 (1877 [C.1891] LXXV1810)
[10] Source: I. G. Whittaker, 1998
[11] See T. E. Brown's poem, Fo'c'sle Yarns

preferring to go into business ashore, though ironically he drowned in an accident off Scarlett Point (on the Isle of Man), while sailing a small boat from Castletown to the regatta at nearby Port St Mary.

For centuries, the Karran family farmed Ballingan farm near the Braaid, a picturesque, rural area in the parish of Marown, ironically the only Manx parish that is landlocked. Traditionally, only one son could make a living from the farm, so it was Thomas' son, John, who took up trade as a saddler in Arbory Street, Castletown. The British economy was booming at this time and the British Government in London had established a garrison of troops in Castletown to prevent a recurrence of the smuggling[12] which had once been rife between the Isle of Man and the rest of Great Britain. This smuggling cost the island its full independence, although the island did not become part of the United Kingdom, but instead operates to this day as a Crown dependency of the UK, retaining its own Parliament and legal system.

John's saddle business prospered, supplying the local market as well as the garrison, and thus he was able to convert an old farmhouse at Scarlett[13] into a handsome Victorian family home, renamed *Seamount*[14]. The family's new home name was a nod to the family's new maritime interests.

John's own sons were educated at Castletown Grammar School and King William's College, Castletown. The eldest son, also named John, set up business in Liverpool dealing in leather goods and, later, in property.

Father and son were therefore in a position to advance money to each boy in turn, so they could each purchase a ship. It was decided that they would pay back the debt in due course, the money then being advanced on to the next son who was old enough to consider taking responsibility for a ship.

One of the sons, George Christian Karran, served four years apprenticeship with Daniel Brocklebank's shipping company of Whitehaven, where he started on March 17, 1871, at the age of sixteen. His salary was £4 for the first year, rising to £5, £6, and £7 respectively over the following three years, totalling £22 for the complete apprenticeship.

On August 21, 1875, after arriving at Liverpool docks from the

[11] See T. E. Brown's poem, Fo'c'sle Yarns
[12] The smuggling boat, Peggy, is on display at the Nautical Museum in Castletown in her original boathouse
[13] Not a reference to the colour but meaning 'flat rock' in Norse
[14] A seamount is an oceanographic feature, a submerged mountain rising from the ocean floor

Far East, George was discharged from the Brocklebank company. Soon afterwards, as Captain George Karran, he became master of his own vessel, the *Rio Grande*.

Brocklebank was only one of a very few shipping lines that sailed throughout the nineteenth and twentieth centuries and could claim to have started as early as 1770, and to have lasted for over two hundred years without loss of independence by merging, or selling out to another line, or worse, going out of business completely.

The 224 ton *Castor* was the first ship of the Brocklebank fleet. Later, as the River Mersey became the great maritime centre of the North West of England, Brocklebank's were registered at Liverpool.

Later still, the company finally succumbed to the rapidly changing world of containerisation and, declining British global influence in 1978, the name was changed to Cunard-Brocklebank for a number of years while Cunard managed a number of shipping lines. However, when the last two Brocklebank ships were sold to a Panamanian owner in 1978, the 208 years of Brocklebank's proud history came to a close.

The Brocklebank house-flag played an interesting part in seafaring history. Of the twenty-six letters of the International Code of Signals (an international system of signals and codes for use by vessels to communicate important messages concerning safety of navigation and related matters), twenty-four are rectangular and two (the letters 'A' and 'B') are 'swallow-tailed'.

'B' is red, and with its distinctive shape and colour, quite outstanding. Flown individually, its message states, 'I am loading, discharging, or carrying dangerous goods'.

'A' is divided vertically into two colours – white and blue (the latter being the 'flying' part). This flag, when hoisted alone, reads, 'I have a diver down' and is used by tender or safety boats when their divers are in the water.

The Brocklebank shipping line's house-flag was white and blue, the same colours as the letter 'A' (although its shape differed as the house-flag was rectangular, not swallow-tailed). Thus, it pre-dated the formation of the International Code, as Brocklebank's started in 1770 and, although naval codes were in use earlier, it was not until the 1880s that a number of countries established their own flag signals.

However, in 1855 the British Board of Trade drafted a system of signals that could be used internationally. The International Code of Signals (ICS) was accepted by almost all countries worldwide.

During World War I, various countries set up their own systems of communications flags, which restricted the value of the older British system. It would be 1932, at the International Radio Telegraphic Conference in Madrid, when discussions were raised concerning radio telegraphic and flag signals, that a new code was agreed by almost all nations.

Various other assemblies have taken place since, but the 1932

code established the signal system that is still in use today.

At some point during this development, the Brocklebank company was approached by one of the above organisations with a request to alter their older house-flag to avoid confusion with the international letter 'A'. Brocklebank's refused. As a result, the shape of the international code flag 'A' was altered to display the distinctive swallow tail.

**Rounding Cape Horn**

# VIOLA
## Built 1869
## 150 Ton

*Viola,* built in Whitehaven in 1869, was sailed and owned by Tom Karran, brother of George. At one hundred and fifty tons she was almost double the size of *Enigma*, and was mainly used for the

Mediterranean trade. She was rigged as a brig and although bigger, was similar to the *Enigma* when she was originally fitted for sea.

# JANE WILLIAMSON

Launched 1870    Sunk by Gunfire 1917
Length 105 feet
Beam 24.2 feet
Draught 13 feet
250 Ton

The two-masted brig, *Jane Williamson* - also owned by Tom Karran - was launched on 17 March, 1870. She was used for trading cargo between the UK and China, through turbulent seas that were navigated by an evidently exceptional crew as the *Jane Williamson* is recorded as having experienced the 'Great Typhoon' of 1880 whilst in the China Seas under Tom's command.

One voyage is recorded to have lasted four and a half years, which is probably the total amount of time that Tom owned her. She was named by the shipbuilders, H & J Williamson, presumably after a member of the Williamson family. Tom sold her to an owner in Belfast and from then on she was used for coastal trading.

It was during World War I - at 4.00 p.m. on 10th September, 1917 - when *Jane Williamson* was twenty miles NNE of St Ives, Cornwall (en route from Liverpool to Cherbourg on the N coast of France with a load of coal), when she was intercepted by a submarine of the Imperial German Navy[15]. The crew of *Jane Williamson* quickly took to the lifeboat, but (as happened so frequently in this war) the U-boat commander did not risk a second's delay in opening fire. The master and three crew were killed, the mate was wounded, and only the ship's boy escaped unharmed as the ship was sunk by gunnery[16]. A trawler picked up the two survivors and took them to Penzance.

[15] British Vessels Lost At Sea (published by HMSO, 1919)
[16] It is not generally appreciated how devastatingly successful the U-boat campaign of WW1 was. It very nearly lost the war for the Allies. Multiple losses occurred on a daily basis and little could be done to counter the U-boat attacks.

Reefing the sail

# RIO GRANDE

c 1880
Length 110 Feet
Beam 24 Feet
Draught 11.6 Feet
200 Ton

The *Rio Grande* was George Karran's first command in 1875. He was only twenty years old when he bought the vessel, having already obtained his Master's Certificate (though he was obliged to carry a sailing master aboard, as maritime law stated that the master of a vessel had to have reached the age of twenty-one).

It is recorded that the *Rio Grande* was trading into ports in northern China that were actually closed to European shipping. The seas around these ports were also notorious for piracy and it was not uncommon for ships' masters and crews to carry aboard boxes of broken glass: the glass would be cast around the decks, particularly at night while the ship was at anchor. When the barefooted 'bogey man' snuck aboard, his presence was quickly exposed.

The *Rio Grande* had ten or twelve old muskets for defence, although there is no record of these ever being used in 'anger'.

Like the *Jane Williamson*, *Rio Grande* also survived the Great Typhoon that bludgeoned the China Seas in 1880. Amazingly, of the eleven ships that the Karran family owned throughout this period of trade, not one of their vessels was lost at sea. However, *Rio Grande* did sustain severe storm damage, enough for the masters of two other ships - who were sailing in the same waters - to be sufficiently concerned to offer to take the *Rio Grande's* crew aboard their own vessels. George Karran steadfastly refused, though he did agree to accept some provisions from the crew of a Norwegian barque, *Mina*. The welcome gifts included molasses, beef and gin which, George later declared, 'put a little life in us.'

During what seemed to be a run of endless days and nights battered by the typhoon, much of the *Rio Grande's* cargo was jettisoned to lighten the ship: the cargo had actually 'shifted to port.' George also recorded how a lot of flotsam had been washed overboard in the storm. This was mostly spars and yards (basically wooden poles), much of which was still attached to the vessel by the rigging. At first, *Rio Grande* was blown along faster than the timber and coir in the sea, but she soon slowed down as her bows were pointing into the monstrous waves, and were therefore being held by the flotsam sea anchor that had inadvertently formed.

When the cyclone finally subsided, the *Rio Grande* was effectively refitted at sea by the master and crew, who sailed back to the British Isles under a jury rig.[17]

[17] The term jury rig - a common term used by sailors - derives from a period when Britain and France were adversaries. Jury was adopted by British sailors from the French word jour or journée (day). Jury rig therefore means day rig, 'a temporary measure to survive a problem or emergency'.

Before the days of radio communication, it was normal for cargo ships arriving from overseas to report for order to their agents, stationed mainly at Falmouth (UK) or Queenstown (Cobh, Ireland). The agents gave instructions as to where to proceed to discharge their cargo.

On arrival at the south of Ireland, George sent a letter to James, one of his six brothers. James had not gone to sea, but instead became a man of the cloth, holding a much respected position as the Reverend Chaplain to Lord Salisbury at Hatfield House in England. The text of Captain George's letter is still in existence, though the original draft was destroyed some sixty years later when his son Tom's house was destroyed by a bomb during the Blitz. The first half of the letter reads:

*My Dear Brother,*

*I was very glad to receive your letter, and also to hear of you all being well. You must thank my nephew for me for his kind offer. We have suffered terribly. Since the first of February we had a succession of hurricanes. We lost bowsprit and jibboom, fore and main top-masts and boats. Nearly all of two suits of sails. I saved one small gig. The Boatswain was washed overboard and had two of his ribs broken, one man crushed, and myself being washed under the windlass and having my ankle hurt. We laid on our beam ends for 18 hours with our yard arms in the water. For 28 or 30 days the sea made a clear breach over the ship fore and aft. Nothing but bread and brackish water, no fire, not able to get a smoke even, we could not get a light with the steam of the cargo. The bulwarks and topgallant rails are gone fore and aft. The crew are in a most pitiable state, covered with sores and so stiff they cannot move. I have had to discharge three of them here, they not being able to proceed to Liverpool. You say you think the Varuna was as bad as us, but the gale he describes and in which he received his damage was nothing to what we had before. He says my boats were all right, but I only had the small gig and no oars.'*[18]

It could be argued that this brief correspondence to James does not paint the *Rio Grande's* master or crew in a favourable light regarding their competence as sailors, but the fact that they survived a month in the adverse conditions described above should, in fact, be a testimony to the calibre of the seamen sailing aboard this brig.

In 1884, *Rio Grande* was sold to R.E. Love of Newcastle, New South Wales.

[18] Mss 77A, Manx Museum, Douglas

Steering in heavy weather

# HOPE

*Built 1858*
*250 Ton*

The *Hope*, built in Prussia in 1858, was the fifth smaller vessel to become part of the Karran fleet. This was one of the ships that John Karran senior purchased, though the master was his son, Tom. The *Hope* had quite a unique feature for a vessel of her tonnage: a centreboard was fitted to her keel in order to reduce her draught (depth) as she would be sailing around the shallow Baltic ports. A centreboard is basically a retractable extension of metal or timber sheet that slides through the keel of a boat, so the boat can more easily grip the water, thus reducing leeway. Tom Karran commented that no crew member had two sets of oilskins, as the sailors' spare clothes would be used to block leaks that came through the centreboard casing. While this basic explanation of a drop keel is sufficient to understand the difficulties faced by master and crew aboard the *Hope*, it is worth noting that, although the principle of sliding a piece of flat timber through the bottom of a vessel has been used for millennia (particularly in some Chinese junks and also rafts in various parts of the world), there is no record of the idea being adapted for the evolution of European boats or ships throughout the ages. However, during America's colonial era, the centreboard idea was developed on the Atlantic seaboard for use in shallow water (such as Chesapeake Bay).

In the late eighteenth century, though, the Royal Navy did experiment with this idea and actually fitted a number of smaller ships with centreboards, though it soon came to be of general opinion that centreboards were in fact a weakness to a ship's strength. However, the principle of the drop keel was taken up by an entrepreneurial Manxman who lived, by coincidence, in Castletown, Isle of Man. His name was George Quayle and it is on record that he was in correspondence with Admiral Schanks of the Royal Navy who was in charge of the Navy's ship design experiments. Consequently, in the 1790's, George Quayle fitted his twenty-six foot boat, *Peggy*, with three sliding keels. The *Peggy* still exists, lying in her original boathouse in Castletown harbour, which has become part of the Manx National Heritage's Nautical Museum.

On Monday 27th August, 1883, the *Hope* was sailing in sight of the Sunda Strait, between Sumatra and Java, when the crew witnessed the volcanic eruption of Krakatoa. The explosion had a force equivalent to over ten thousand times the atom bomb which destroyed Hiroshima in 1945, and was heard almost three thousand miles away near Mauritius. Krakatoa's volcanic explosion caused the deaths of thirty-six thousand people and thousands more were injured by tsunamis and falling lava, as well as the sulphur dioxide gas that choked the air. The *Hope* survived, evidently having been far enough away from the eruption not to have been directly impacted.

In 1886, *Hope* was sold to an Argentinean ship owner.

At sea in a gale

Good Sailing

# SUMATRA

*Built 1858    Wrecked 1901*
*Length 172.4 Feet   Beam 32 Feet*
*Draught 20.8 Feet  773 Ton*

In 1858, when the *Hope* was being built in Prussia, another vessel, the *Sumatra*, was being constructed at Whitehaven, Cumberland, by *T & J Brocklebank & Co*. She was to join the Brocklebank fleet, trading mainly between the U.K. and Calcutta.

Her overall general measurements show that she was not large, but this timber hulled vessel, with three masts, was a full rigged ship.

In 1876, John Karran bought the *Sumatra*, his son Tom taking command as Master. *Sumatra* can be regarded as the family's first step towards sailing the bigger ships that they would obtain in later years of the fleet's history.

In 1884, after eight years of service with the Karran fleet, *Sumatra* was sold to a company in Montevideo, Uruguay, and renamed *Clara B*. She then changed hands eleven years later, when she was purchased by a company registered at Oslo, Norway. Her new owners shortened her name to *Clara*.

**Working Aloft**

On 19th January, 1901, she was abandoned by her Norwegian crew.[19] Research into details of her loss have proved fruitless by this author, but further investigation into the subject revealed that the master and crew of the Liverpool steamship, *Ardova*, received awards in recognition of their services in rescuing the crew of the abandoned barque, *Clara*. As a result, some crew members of the *Ardova* received accolades from the Norwegian Government: Captain Smith received a binocular glass; the First Mate and two seamen were each presented with a silver medal and diploma[20].

Incidentally, a painting depicting the *Sumatra* was used on a Manx postage stamp in 1984.

[19] Source: The Times, 1st February, 1901
[20] Source: The Times, 3rd July, 1901

# MANX QUEEN

From Captain George's collection, possibly a sister ship to the Manx Queen

*Built 1878    Lost 1902*
*317 Ton*

Manx Queen

The *Manx Queen* was an iron barque, built in 1878 by *Noble & Co.* at Barrow-in-Furness for Robert Karran,[21] brother of George and Tom.

Whilst *Sumatra* was the first of the vessels of larger tonnage to be owned by the Karran family, *Manx Queen* can be regarded as one of intermediate size, being larger than five of the fleet's vessels, yet still smaller than the five bigger barques and ships. Her master, Robert, was as proud of *Manx Queen* as any of the other vessels, perhaps because she was particularly fast.

On one occasion, when *Manx Queen* was moored alongside a pier at San Francisco, it became apparent that the cargo to be loaded in her cargo-hold would have to be protected from the ship's frames (the ribs to which the vessel's sides were riveted). In such a scenario, the normal procedure is to line the frames with timber (the timber generally known today as 'cargo battens', although *Manx Queen's* crew referred to it as 'scantling wood'). To obtain such timber for the *Manx Queen* would have cost precious time and money, which Captain Robert would have been keen to avoid. Fortuitously, the Chief Officer stepped in and assured Robert that he would have the job done and the ship loaded in no time, providing that there was no interference and that he was left to simply get on with loading the ship. Captain Robert agreed, the Chief Officer soon completed the task, and *Manx Queen* left port. However, several days after leaving 'Frisco, Captain Robert finally succumbed to curiosity and asked the mate where he had procured the scantling wood. The mate replied, 'Well, Captain, you know that pier we were tied up to…?' (He had removed some of the planking from underneath the jetty's double decking and lined the cargo hold with the wood). Unfortunately, Captain Robert's reply to this revelation is not on record.

In 1889, when *Manx Queen* was eleven years old, she was sold to *Wm Jarvis & Sons*, Liverpool, and registered as *The Manx Queen Co.* Three years later, she changed hands again to the *British & Mexican Shipping Co. Ltd. Manx Queen* was evidently a successful trader as this company sailed her for ten years. Sadly though, on 4th February, 1902, whilst on a passage from Laguna, Brazil, to Falmouth, England, she was abandoned. Research by this author to find the reason, or the *Manx Queen's* geographical position, has proved unsuccessful to date.

In Port (New York)

# McDIARMID

*Built 1883   Broken up 1928*
*Length 255 Feet*
*Beam 38 Feet*
*Draught 22 Feet*
*1622 Gross Ton    1568 Net Ton*

*McDiarmid* was the last ship to be purchased by the Karran family, though not the last to be sold. In 1883, when the crew of the *Hope* was observing the colossal eruption of Krakatoa, the *McDiarmid* was being built in the shipyard of *A. McMillan & Co* in Dumbarton, on the River Clyde. The ship was named after *McMillan's* foreman, Archie McDiarmid.

In 1886, the *McDiarmid* was sold to a Palermo ship owner. Later, in 1901, she was bought by Captain George Karran.

In 1907, the ship was on passage from New South Wales to

**Decks awash**

Chile when she lost a mast in storm conditions. Fortunately, she made Auckland, New Zealand, for repairs.

In 1910, after only nine years service as part of the Karran fleet, the *McDiarmid* was sold to a company based at Genoa. *McDiarmid* had entered service with the Karran fleet when British shipping was sadly starting to encounter something of a recession. She changed hands again in 1919 when another Genoan company purchased her. Finally, in 1928, after forty-six years of maritime service, *McDiarmid* was sold to Italian breakers.

# IMBERHORNE

Built 1882    Sunk by Enemy Action 1917
Length 284.1 Feet
Beam 41.2 Feet
2042 Gross Tons

In 1882, *Imberhorne*, a full rigged ship, was built by *A. McMillan & Co* of Dumbarton, for Mr. Price of Imberhorne Manor in Sussex. *W. R. Price & Co.* sailed her until 1895 when she joined the Karran fleet. Her tonnage would make her the largest ship in the Karran fleet, and possibly the largest in the British Merchant Navy at the time.

When the Karran family purchased her, Captain Harry Lever took command of the vessel. Examples of her voyages include May to September, 1905, from Hamburg to Sydney (in 112 days), then Australia to South America with a cargo of coal (in 72 days) and back to Sydney in 1906 (in 95 days). In 1907 she carried a cargo of nitrates from the Pacific coast of South America to Great Britain in four and a half months.

The *Imberhorne* was well-fitted, with cabins amidship, and the crew accommodated aft where there would be much more comfort at sea, instead of being for'd (forward) in the foc'sle, where there would be much more motion, plus flooding in heavy weather. Another comfort was a bridge that ran the length of the ship, enabling the crew to be above the sea swept decks for much of the time. (It is interesting to note that later, this type of bridge would become more commonly known to sailors as a 'flying bridge' and, because of their low freeboard, would be much used in the design of oil tankers).

During these years, Captain Lever's wife, Monica, usually travelled with him on long voyages, and their children were born at sea. Later, Captain Lever left the employment of the Karran Fleet to take command of a steamship, *Wirral* (of Liverpool). Sadly, shortly after transferring to the *Wirral*, this well-respected man died.

Lever was replaced by Castletown man, Dick Stowell, who became *Imberhorne*'s new Master. Stowell, like Lever before him, was held in high esteem by his employers, particularly as he was exceptionally talented at mathematics and navigation.

In 1911, Captain George Karran sold the *Imberhorne* when she was twenty-nine years old. Her new owners were Salvesen & Co. of Leith, Scotland[22].

In 1907, Salvesen & Co. ventured into the Antarctic whaling business, using New Island (in the Falkland's Archipelago) as a base. A lease was then obtained to use South Georgia as a depot. This station in Stromness Bay, South Georgia, was named Leith Harbour by Salvesen & Co.

Two ships *Glengown* and *Sabina*, had been discarded at the Falklands in the 1890s and were subsequently acquired by Salvesen &

Co. who arranged for them to be moved to South Georgia station, where they were then used as warehouses for storing products such as whale oil, whale bone, and the valuable fertilizer, guano. When Salvesen & Co. obtained *Imberhorne* from the Karran family, they intended to use her as a warehouse hulk at Leith harbour, but she sailed so excellently from Great Britain to South Georgia that her new owners decided to give her a new lease of life, using her to ship their products to Europe. By 1909, all of Salvesen & Co.'s vessels were steamships, the exception being *Imberhorne*.

Later, *Imberhorne* was damaged when leaving Princess Dock, Glasgow. As a result, a decision was made to sell her. On 4th March, 1913, her final owner became R. Mattson of Mariehamn, Åland Islands, Finland. Indeed, the Åland Island ship owners bought quite a number of sailing ships, often when times were quiet or bordering on recession.

These Åland Island sailors were often considered amongst the best in the business, and were amongst the last to sail this type of commercial ship. However, by the late 1930s, even these die-hard mariners had to go over to the use of steam.

*Imberhorne's* new master was Captain Isidor Eriksson, a native of the Åland Islands. Aged forty, he had twenty-three years sea experience behind him.
In July 1916, *Imberhorne* nearly came to grief when she drifted ashore during loading in Pascagoula, USA, when the port was hit by a hurricane. Fortunately she was refloated without much damage

The end of *Imberhorne* came on 1st May, 1917, whilst en route from Mobile, Alabama, to the Clyde in Scotland with a load of timber. The ship was intercepted by a German submarine, the U.73. Karran family records read: 'sunk off Irish coast', although a separate account in the Karran archives state that the vessel was 130 Nautical Miles North West by West "of [sic] Stags of Broadhaven, Mobile for Clyde, Pitchpine." The precise fix given in this distance and bearing from the County Mayo rocks can thus be accepted .

*Imberhorne's* former Master, Captain Isidor Eriksson, did not perish with his ship. Eleven years later, in 1928, he took charge of another ship, *The Kastleholm*. Later, in 1942, *The Kastleholm* was torpedoed in the Atlantic. Once again the amazingly fortunate Eriksson survived another encounter with the German Navy and continued his career at sea until the age of seventy-two.

# LADY ELIZABETH

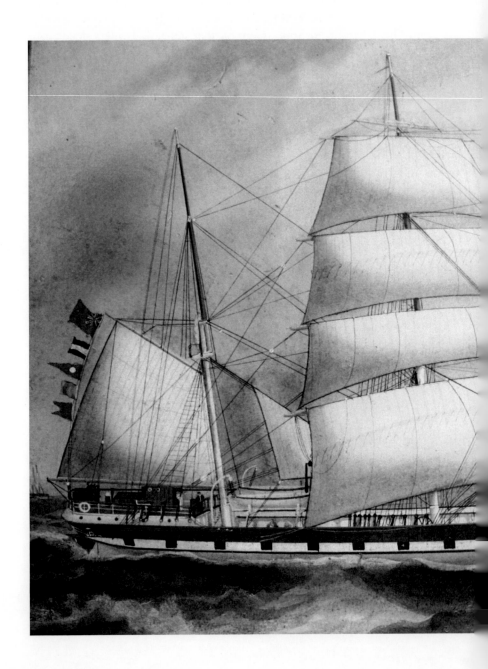

*Built 1879   Declared Unseaworthy 1913*
*Length 223 Feet   Beam 35 Feet   Draught 21.4 Feet*
*1208 Gross Tons    1155 Net Tons*

The *Lady Elizabeth* was an iron barque, built in 1879 by Robert Thomson, Southwick, Sunderland, for J. Wilson and was registered in London.

In 1880, when Captain George Karran brought *Rio Grande* back to the Irish Sea after the Great Typhoon, his ability as a ship-master had been well tested and his thoughts, undoubtedly, had turned to procuring a vessel of much larger tonnage. Indeed, it is likely – though not confirmed – that before long he sold *Rio Grande* at Dunedin, New Zealand, the place where, on a previous visit, he had also fallen in love with Matilda (Tilly) May Wolfe Clark. George was now twenty-eight years old and his fiancée, Tilly, was eighteen and deemed old enough to be married. After travelling as passengers to George's home of Castletown, the happy couple were given a very warm welcome at Seamount (the Karran family home). It was also around this time that George obtained the other lady in his life: the *Lady Elizabeth*.

Although *Lady Elizabeth* was generally a standard barque, she was fitted with the passenger service from Great Britain to India in mind. Her cabins were fitted in maple wood and had brass fittings (cast iron fittings would have sufficed on a lesser vessel). Her original log-book would tell of voyages such as North Shields to Bombay (carrying 1760 tons of coal) and Madras to London (carrying brown sugar from palm sap). On other trips the cargo was Nux Vomica (the seed of an Indian tree used as strychnine poison) and deer horns.

The *Lady Elizabeth*'s Master, George Karran, lost no time in getting to sea with his newly acquired

**Lady Elizabeth (with original 4 masts)**

58

ship, leaving London on 29th January, 1884, arriving at Sydney on 25th May. His log recorded that on 23rd February, after only twenty-five days at sea, the mainsail fores, two lower topsails, fore topmast and mizzen stay sails were all blown away in hurricane force winds. Futhermore, the bulwarks on both sides of the poop were stove in and the vessel was then 'hove to' under close reefed canvas. On 24th March, in another violent storm, more damage occurred, as well as flooding in the accommodation.

The ports of call on this voyage would be Newcastle (New South Wales), Valparaiso (Chile), Queenstown (Ireland) for orders, Greenock (Scotland) for a pilot, and on to Glasgow. At Sydney, six seamen had left the ship. Whether able-seaman, William Leech, a sixty-year old Belfast man, joined her then, or if he was one of the crew that had sailed on the passage from London, is not known but, sadly, this sailor died after a fall from aloft on 11th September 1884, two weeks before the ship arrived at Valparaiso.

George's new wife, Tilly, must have had a strong personality and excellent sea-legs for as long as her husband was at sea, she remained at his side despite all disasters.

On 3rd May, 1888, three miles off the Chilean port of Pisagua, Tilly gave birth to their first child who they named Thomas William (after his uncle, Captain T.W. Karran). The port's local nurse, who could only speak a Spanish Peruvian dialect, wrapped baby Tom so tightly in swaddling clothes that he resembled an Egyptian mummy. When Tilly saw this she was horrified: she thought the child had died and was wrapped in a shroud. Fortunately, the English doctor and nurse, who had been upcountry, promptly arrived and soon the infant was dressed European style. Little Tom

**The Old Lady**

quickly became quite a celebrity in the eyes of the ship's crew, as well as the local Chilean people.

It is likely that George would have given the order to 'splice the mainbrace', a Royal Navy term used by sailors to refer an extra ration of rum to celebrate a job well done or a special event. However, it is unlikely that any festivities involving alcohol would get too out-of-hand on Captain George's vessel. He was a God-fearing man and when docked in isolated ports, such as Pisagua, his ship became something of a mini chapel, where sailors from other vessels would come aboard to join in with prayers and hymns.

Just over a year later, *Lady Elizabeth* made another visit to South America and, on picking up the pilot for entering harbour, George was

informed that another Manx ship, *Manx King*, had recently called there and that the Captain of that ship had died and been buried at sea.

George must have been devastated: the dead man was Captain Robert Karran, his brother. An entry in *Manx King's* log, dated 19th July, 1889 (the day of Robert's death) read: 'On this day we committed the body of our beloved and trusted Captain to the sea'. The Chief Officer of the ship had assumed command, taking the *Manx King* from South America to Great Britain.

All following voyages made by these two ships would see Captain George Karran as Master of the *Manx King*, with newly-appointed Captain Cannell as Captain of the *Lady Elizabeth*.

By the turn of the twentieth century, almost ninety-five percent of British ships departing U.K. ports were steam-powered, and the figure for foreign tonnage using steam was over eighty percent.

With sail declining, it was decided (in 1906) that the *Lady Elizabeth* would be sold. The new owners were the Norwegian company, Skibsakies Elskabet.

The new company's manager, Mr. L. Lydersen, had a fleet of ships quite similar to those of the Karran family, but the Norwegian vessels were each registered as an individual company.

BR. SHIP "LADY ELIZABETH,,
CAPT. KARRAN & OFFICERS.

On 4th December, 1912, *Lady Elizabeth* left Vancouver with a cargo of timber, bound for Delagoa Bay, Lourenco Marques, Mozambique. Once again, the notorious seas south of Cape Horn would try to claim another vessel and, in the event, the *Lady Elizabeth* - and much of the deck cargo - was badly damaged and the lifeboats lost overboard. However, although in a very distressed condition, on 12th March, 1913, the ship somehow managed to reach the Falkland Islands. Unfortunately, when trying to negotiate the narrow channel into Port Stanley's natural harbour, she struck the Uranie Rock, near Volunteer Point. (The fact that this rock was named after the French frigate, L'Uranie, who came to grief there in 1820, gives some indication of the rock's danger).

The *Lady Elizabeth* succeeded in making it into Port Stanley, although she had taken in a lot of water. A diver surveyed the hull, finding she had been holed when striking the rock and had also broken her keel. She was therefore declared unseaworthy and subsequently sold to the Falkland Island Company.

For the next twenty-three years, *Lady Elizabeth* served as a storage warehouse for the company. In 1936, she blew adrift in a storm and grounded about one and a quarter miles from Port Stanley, at Whalebone Cove (51° South/57 ° West). And there she lies to this day. In 1970, she was surveyed at the same time as the *S.S. Great Britain*, but it was concluded that any disturbance to the sandbar that had formed around the *Lady Elizabeth* would cause extreme stress and even more damage to her hull. Therefore, it was decided that only the *Great Britain* would be brought back to Britain. Now, four decades later, the *Great Britain* has almost been refitted to her former glory, a credit to all concerned. She is docked at Bristol where she is open to the general public as a museum.

Almost a century after the *Lady Elizabeth* was abandoned at Port Stanley, she still lies at Whalebone Cove. Her iron hull plating is still intact, but rust has steadily taken its toll. Her three lower masts are still in their original position. The *Lady Elizabeth* is said to be the most imposing of the many wrecks that litter the Falkland's coastline.

Interestingly, in Tessa Karran's memoirs, she notes that before she was born, the *Lady Elizabeth* had sailed into Port Stanley with cargo that would be used to build the Island's tabernacle church. This church is still in use today. One can only wonder how many people, Falklanders included, know of this strange connection between the church and the abandoned barque.

The Lady Elizabeth at Capetown, S.A.

# MANX KING

*Built 1884    Sunk by U-Boat 1918*
*Length 251 Feet    Beam 39 Feet    Draught 24 Feet*
*Gross Tonnage 1751    Nett Tonnage 1702*

On 4th October, 1884, the *Manx King*, an iron ship, was launched by *Richardson, Duck & Co.* at Stockton-on-Tees for Captain Robert Karran. She had cabins that were quite luxurious, the ship's interior designers having taken into account the need for passenger comfort on long journeys to far-flung destinations in the Indian Ocean.

On her stern the *Manx King* proudly displayed the Manx crest, the Three Legs of Man. For'd, her figurehead was that of a Viking king who once ruled the island, King Orry.

Robert's Chief Officer was J. Cannell of Douglas, and crew members included William Mounsey and sailors Green, Kelly, Cain, Kinrade, Costain and Kerruish.

We can accept that she was a 'happy' ship, and remained so after Captain Robert's death in the Pacific (off South America) in 1889.

The following year, George took command of the *Manx King*, a station he would hold for the next sixteen years. Always with him aboard were his wife, Tilly, their daughter, Tessa, and son, Tom. On 24th December 1892, in the North Atlantic, another son, Jack, was born. The latitude and longitude co-ordinates read: 04.16° North, 24° 31' West.

The children spent their childhood at sea. Later, at the outbreak

of the Great War, the boys signed up as officers in the Army. Aged twenty-two, as a Captain of the South Wales Borderers, Jack lost his life at the Battle of the Somme. His brother Tom suffered severe shell shock in the trenches in Northern France. As for Tessa, after spending almost sixteen years at sea as a child, she settled down at Castletown, becoming Mrs. Kinvig, the wife of a much-respected school teacher. Before passing away in 1974 (aged 83), Tessa penned her memoirs which give an insight into this extraordinary lifestyle, describing the unique features of living aboard a ship. For example, she relates how the ship's carpenter would make toys for the children, including a toy house (later generations would call such a plaything a 'wendy house') and a much loved sledge. The sailors, no doubt, had many laughs watching the youngsters sliding up and down the deck, in tune to the ship's motion. The sailors then followed suit, producing playthings for the children: dolls, skipping ropes, and swings made from rope-line. Such toys were works of art as the sailors had advanced skills in rope work.

'School lessons' were held in the chart room, not the 'bell to bell' routine of school-life ashore. However, the lessons were certainly as productive. 'Class' times fitted around the particular lesson to hand, rather than the instruction period lasting a definite time.

As they grew up, another lady joined the three women (Tilly, Tessa and the carpenter's wife) onboard. The Chief Officer Pratt's daughter, Constance, was taken on as governess, giving the children another excellent role model. By the time Tessa had reached the age of fourteen, she could speak six languages, and her two brothers were equally well-educated.

Tessa also records the high regard she had for the officers and crew of the ship. Once, when the ship was docked in Rio de Janeiro, Tessa contracted yellow fever, endemic on the coast at the time. She wrote that every 'man jack turned to', assisting with the cargo handling etc. so that the ship could be ready to sail in record time. It took Tessa months to recover to full strength again, but no crew member ever complained of the risks associated with carrying a diseased passenger aboard. She also recorded the irony in the fact that, years later, Rio de Janeiro had become a South American health resort!

Tessa's records also include stories of severe weather conditions, describing how the imminent arrival of a typhoon or hurricane would be announced to the ship's navigators by a sudden fall of the barometer reading.

At night, the children would congregate in their mother's cabin. Constance would make cocoa while Tilly read aloud. In the comfortable, warm saloon, they would hear the ship labouring as it rolled in heavy seas, the timber joints and fastenings constantly creaking and groaning.

The Master of *Manx King*, George Karran, and Chief Officer Pratt would find a moment to visit the cabin at the children's bedtime. Their wet oilskins would shine in the lamp light. Each man had an axe tucked into his rope-belt that was tied around his waist , the axes were vital as the axes were vital in cutting away any timber spars or ropes that had 'carried away' from their positions). 'Ties' around the men's ankles and cuffs helped to keep them as dry as possible. The term used by sailors to

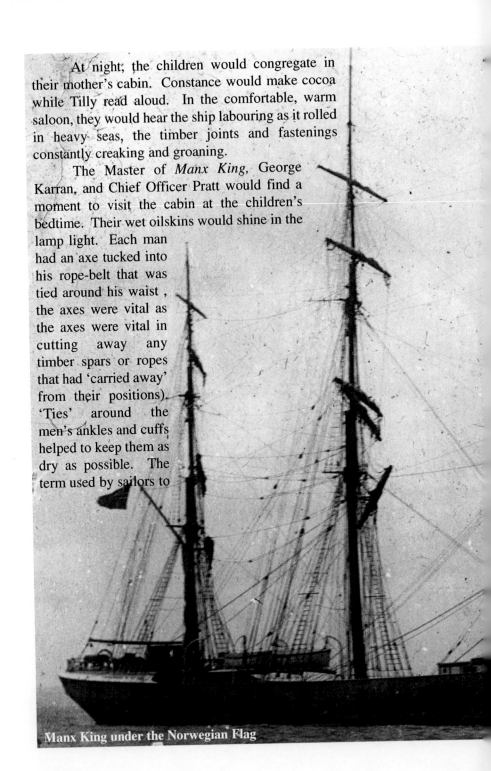

Manx King under the Norwegian Flag

describe this self-rigged attire was 'body and soul lashings' – a tongue-in-cheek phrase. Many a seaman must have owed his life to such canny dress sense, as he stood much less chance of being blown overboard like a kite.

Another remarkable incident preserved in Tessa's maritime accounts includes an incident that took place in the port of Dunkirk. *Manx King*, being moored in this port, was flying her usual flag, the British Red Ensign (often affectionately referred to as the 'Red Duster'). Manx vessels, however, would display the Three Legs of Man in the 'flying' part of the flag. (A painting in the Manx Museum, Isle of Man, depicts a brig in the Bay of Naples in 1788 flying a blue ensign 'defaced' with the triskele, the Isle of Man's three legged symbol). Subsequently, it would appear that this tradition was never endorsed by Britain's Parliament, although in the early 1980's this was amended: now the Isle of Man Shipping Register is amongst the most respected in the world, and all of the ships on this register fly the Manx red ensign as described.

At Dunkirk, however, the British Consul boarded the *Manx King*, demanding the ensign be taken down. The ship's Master, George Karran, refused, ordering the Consul ashore. Seeking a compromise, a message was 'wired' to George's brother, the Reverend James Karran, who was the Chaplain to Lord Salisbury at Hatfield House in England (an esteemed site in English heritage, Hatfield House was also the place where Queen Elizabeth 1 was informed that she had become Queen of England). At this time, Lord Salisbury held the position of 'Premier' (Prime Minister) and his return message to the Consul read: 'Leave the Manxman alone, let him fly his flag.'

It must have been a great day for the Manx men at Dunkirk.

Only a few decades later, in 1940, during World War II, a fleet of cross-channel passenger ships belonging to the Isle of Man Steam Packet Company were requisitioned to join the small and capital ships for 'Operation Dynamo', often simply referred to as 'Dunkirk'. Tessa would have been forty-nine years old then, and undoubtedly would have been extremely saddened to hear that three of the Steam Packet's fine ships were lost at Dunkirk - along with many other vessels - causing a huge loss of life to crew members and servicemen.

One of the Steam Packet's fated ships was named after the same Manx Norse King as the Karran vessel, *Manx King* (though the Steam Packet's ship had a more definitive moniker: *King Orry*).

The *King Orry* had seen much service in her lifetime and, apart from the usual peacetime passenger trade, she endured virtually all of the First World War in the Northern waters of the British Isles, after being fitted out as a 'boarding ship' and patrolling the often storm-tossed seas, intercepting and searching vessels of all sizes for signs of contraband. For sometime she was disguised as a cargo trader, her name altered to *Viking Orry*, a ruse to misleadingly suggest a Norwegian identity.

Her contribution to the war effort, so briefly mentioned here, does not really do her justice, but one incident is always remembered by Manx people: in November 1918, after the Armistice, the surrendered German warships were ordered to report to British warships at arranged positions. On 21st November, fourteen of these capital ships of the German High Seas Fleet were intercepted and escorted into the Firth of Forth on the east coast of Scotland. When the British ships took position amongst the German fleet, Admiral Beatty gave *King Orry* 'pride of place' by giving her orders to be positioned centre of the ships passing signals onto the fleet (such as alterations of course or speed). Amazingly, *King Orry* was the only representative of the British or allied Merchant Navies present.

On 29th May 1940, the *King Orry* was back in action, but this time fate was not so kind to her: she was bombed at sea, near Dunkirk, finally sinking in the early hours of 30th May.

In an excerpt from a letter that was published in the much respected nautical magazine, *Sea Breezes*, Mr Robert Randic explained that he joined the *Manx King* at Antwerp on 11th June, 1909, as an ordinary seaman, alongside Captain Cannell (Master), Mr Sword (mate) and Mr Nash (second mate). There were fourteen men 'before the mast', a term used to mean that sailors were housed for'd (in the front of the ship), in front of the masts. Mr. Randic also stated that, 'The master's wife also went to sea with us.' He went on:

'As usual we tacked in the Channel for several days, had an uneventful crossing of the line [Equator] and run way down to Staten Island which we passed in full view. On September 1st, the ship ran into foul weather off the Horn and it was not till October 2nd that we gained enough westerly longitude enabling us to turn north. True to Manx tradition, under the ship's counter was the appropriate emblem, a motto: "Throw me on my feet – I stand still."[23]

'Doldrums on the Pacific side were unusually trying, we were placed on short rations, and the fresh water became unpalatable. Exhausted, we made San Pedro on November 26th, after 169 days under way. When alongside 10 sailors took French leave and were substituted by seven beachcombers. We made Astoria in 18 days falling in with the ill-fated Matterhorn (which had a shifting grain cargo) outward bound at Columbo Bar.

'After being laid up in Portland for 3 months we began loading Oregon spruce for Port Adelaide.

'However I changed ship prior to her sailing in April 1910...one of the apprentices had an unfortunate fall from the forecastle-head onto a log alongside the ship and was killed, another whose indentures expired, left for the state of Montana.

'Friends told me of seeing the Manx King in Montevideo. I spotted her again in August 1917 in New York's lower bay, then under the Norwegian flag.'

In 1911, Captain George Karran decided to sell the Manx King. The new owner was Eduard Ericksen, who was based at Per Mandal near the southern tip of Norway. The ship then changed hands again in 1915 to J. Johannsen Farsund, also in the South of Norway. Her final owners were T. Wilhelms and A. Jacobsen of Fredrikstad, their company registered as Akties, who purchased the Manx King in 1916.

A chance meeting by this author in Castletown, 2007, enlightened me to the details of the actual loss of the Manx King. Peter Karran, none other than the great-grandson of Captain George Christian Karran, introduced himself to me and I had the great privilege of being asked to Seamount, the family home.

---

[23] Author's note - correct translation from Latin: 'Whichever way you throw me, I stand.'

Amongst other documents etc that Mr. Karran showed me, there was a copy of the report from the ship's master to the ship's owner describing the loss of the Manx King:

## The Sinking of 'Manx King' on 8th July 1918
*Report by the captain, Rasmus Emil Halvorsen*
*(translated from Norwegian)*

We left New York sunday [sic] 23 June 1918 with general cargo (iron, cotton, soda, and oil) for Rio de Janeiro. The journey continued with winds from SE, cruising. Nothing special to note before monday [sic] 8th July when the wind went SSW with showers. We sailed towards SE. At 12.00 noon we heard a shot, and a grenade took the water and exploded just aft of the ship with shells flying around the vessel; one fell on the poop. Another shot followed. We stopped, and all hands were called on deck. We then saw a submarine straight forward. The boats were launched and were at the level of the deck when the submarine fired a third shot. The boats were immidiately [sic] lowered and we rowed towards the submarine, where the 1st rate's boat arrived first.

The captain of the submarine asked about the destination of the ship; the answer was Rio de Janeiro. On the question about the cargo the answer was: general cargo. When the captain's boat arrived, the submarine's captain asked for all the ship's paper. Some of these had been left on board and the captain's boat was therefore towed back to the ship.

Eleven men from the submarine went on board in the lifeboat and were ordered to enter the ship with bombs and axes. The captain (of "Manx King") asked the officer from the U-boat if they really intended to sink the ship, to which he answered: "Yes, since it is bound for Rio with contrabande." On board he took all the ship's papers. The captain protested against the sinking, but to no avail. The men from the U-boat took the port lifeboat from the forcastle and launched. Thereafter they started breaking up the hatches and placed bombs in the cargo.

The captain was firmly ordered to abandon the ship immidiately [sic]. We rowed away and hoisted sails together with the mate's boat. The weather looked threathening [sic] so we decided to sail away at once since we could do nothing more for the ship. We agreed to sail WNW, hoping to meet a steamship which could take us on board. After 27 hours in the lifeboats we were rescued by S/S "Anchites" of Liverpool. We were very well treated on board that ship and landed in New York on 14 July 1918. Our crew were 19 men.

Another record given to me by Peter and Rob Karran is shown below.

**New York Times, 13th July, 1918**

# STOPPED BY U-BOAT IN NORTH ATLANTIC; Crew of Norwegian Bark Set Adrift in Small Boats 300 Miles Off Cape Race. DID NOT SEE VESSEL SUNK Survivors Pulled Away While It Was Still Afloat— May Be Converted Into a Raider.

AN ATLANTIC PORT, July 12.—A German submarine, appearing 300 miles off Cape Race on July 6, captured the Norwegian bark Manx King and ordered the crew of nineteen to take to the boats, it was learned tonight when the survivors were brought here on a British steamship, which picked them...

It is heart-warming to note that the crew of both the *Imberhorne* and the *Manx King* all survived after almost identical life-threatening incidents where the odds were stacked against them[24].

Since our introduction to the Karran fleet, starting with the birth of baby Tessa aboard the *Manx King* in storm conditions near Cape Horn (the family fleet by then, in 1891, had already been trading for over thirty years), the story has come full circle, ending up with the details of the loss of this fine ship in the Atlantic.

      Throughout our armchair voyages we have read of the strength of character, leadership and loyalty of the crew members who sailed

[24] British Vessels Lost At Sea - published HMSO 1919 records the staggering number of vessels lost frequently with loss of life. Manx King's loss is not recorded as she was by that time a Norwegian vessel

aboard the vessels of the Karran fleet. Inspiring this leadership throughout was Tessa's father, Captain George Karran.

In 1903, after many years of impeccable seafaring, Captain George Karran finally retired. For the next twenty-five years, he was an active member of the Castletown community (elected to Castletown Commissioners in 1910, and becoming a Magistrate in 1911).

An article in *The Isle of Man Times*, dated Saturday 18th October, 1930, reported that Captain George had died earlier that month, aged 76. The article was headlined: WHEN THE MANX FLAG WAS CARRIED THROUGH THE WORLD. The headline also echoed the words of the Prime Minister, Lord Salisbury to the British Consul at Dunkirk, 'Leave the Manxman alone, let him fly his flag.'

# Acknowledgments

The author is grateful to the following for
their help and support.

My daughter, **Janette Stowell**, who unintentionally acted
as my secretary with the use of her typing skills and
previous publication experience.

**Rob and Peter Karran** for their input of family details,
and photographic images included in this book.

**Captain Sven-Erik Nylund** of Vantaa, Finland, for
information supplied regarding the ship Imberhorne.

**Mrs Maggie Burley** of Putney, London, for details of the
*Imberhorne* from the records researched by her late
husband, **Ken,** who sadly passed away in 1999.

**Captain Allan Bridson**, Merchant Navy (retired) of
Douglas, Isle of Man.

**Mr John Qualtrough**, Manx nautical history enthusiast
of Port St Mary.

**Mr Frank James** for his general support.

**Manx National Heritage** for assisting with the scanning
of Photographic Images.

Not forgetting the scores of friends and
acquaintances who have given me
snippets of information included here.


*Billy Stowell, Isle of Man, 2010*